The Practical Guide to
Teshuvah

The Practical Guide to
Teshuvah

by
Rabbi S. Wagschal

translated from the Hebrew by
Moshe Schapiro

Targum / Feldheim

First published 1991

Copyright © 1991 by Rabbi S. Wagschal
ISBN 0-944070-32-9

Phototypeset at Targum Press

Published by:
Targum Press Inc.
22700 W. Eleven Mile Rd.
Southfield, Mich. 48034

in conjunction with:
Mishnas Rishonim

Distributed by:
Feldheim Publishers
200 Airport Executive Park
Spring Valley, N.Y. 10977

Distributed in Israel by:
Nof Books Ltd.
POB 23646
Jerusalem 91235

Printed in Israel

מתוך ההסכמות שנתקבלו על ספר "בן הישיבה"
מאת הגאון רבי יצחק יעקב וייס (שליט"א) זצ"ל
בעמח"ס שו"ת "מנחת יצחק"
גאב"ד לכל מקהלות האשכנזים עיה"ק ירושלים תובב"א

איקלע לאתרן קדישא ת"י הרה"ג חו"ב מוה"ר **שאול ווגשאל**
שליט"א מגייטסהעד (ענגלאנד) אשר בידעי ומכירי קאמינא רבות
בשנים אשר כבר איתמחי גברא לזכות הרבים בהרבצת תורה
בספריו לסדר אורחת חיים בהליכות עולם אלו ההלכות השכיחות
בכל בתי ישראל מידי יום ביומו ועכשיו בא לכאן ותלמודו בידו אשר
ראה וחקר וידע מן הנסיון כמחנך ממדריגה ראשונה לבוא בדברים
הנכנסים אל הלב של צעירי הצאן תלמידי הישיבות לקחת אותם
בדברים המתיישבים על דעתם בסגנון שהם מבינים כדי למשכם
לתורה ויראת שמים ולהאיר עיניהם במאור התורה אשר בעזה"י
ילכו לאורה כל הימים ואמינא לפעלא טבא יישר שחפץ ד' בידו
יצליח וכל המזכה הרבים זכות הרבים תלוי בו, ונזכה כולנו שיתקיים
הבטחת הנביא ומלאה הארץ דיעה את ה' בביאת גוא"צ בבי"א.
ע"ז בעה"ח יום ג' לסדר והודעתי את חקי הא' וגו' שנת השביעית
תש"מ לפ"ק,

יצחק יעקב וייס
אב"ד פעה"ק ת"ו

הרב ש. וולבה

מנהל רוחני

בישיבת באר יעקב

ב"ה, ב' שבט תש"מ.

דורנו דור עני הוא, ואין עני אלא בדעת: דברים שבעבר הבין כל
בר בי רב מדעתו מבלי שיצטרכו להדריכו בהם, אינם מובנים היום
מאליהם. מוטל, איפוא, על המחנכים להדריך את התלמידים מהצעד
הראשון לתוך עולם התורה בדברים ברורים, ולהעמידם על יסודות
איתנים בדרכם לחיי תורה.

והנה דווקא היום, שהחינוך וההדרכה כה חיוניים הם לכל בן
תורה כאויר לנשימה, נמצא החינוך באיזה ישיבות במצב עגום: ישנן
ישיבות בלי מחנך, ויש ישיבות שלמחנכים אין המעמד המגיע להם
כדי שיהיו דבריהם נשמעים לעבודתו ית'.

במצב זה יש לברך את הרב הג' מוהר"ר **שאול וגשל** שליט"א,
אשר כבר יצאו לו מוניטין כמחנך בחסד עליון, שעמד על צורך
השעה וחיבר קונטרס "לבן הישיבה", בו הוא לוקח את בן־הישיבה
הצעיר בדברים נעימים ומובנים היטב, עוזר לו להתמצא בעולם
התורה, מיעץ לו ומחזקו כיד ה' הטובה עליו. בסגנון הספר ובתוכן
פרקיו ניכר, שהמחבר שליט"א הוא מחנך דגול ובר־סמכא. אין ספק,
כי הקונטרס יעזור לצעירים רבים להכנס לישיבה ברגל ישרה ולקבל
עליהם באהבה את עול התורה, אף שההתחלה קשה וכאשר יערב
להם לאחר מכן, יהי' בזה חלק נכבד לקונטרס זה.

יזכה המחבר הנכבד לזכות את הרבים בעוד ספרים מועילים
ונחוצים כזה!

שלמה וולבה

Preface

THIS BOOK IS designed for those seeking guidance in how to approach the month of Elul and the High Holy Days. Many people find themselves at a loss—how can they, in a few days, transform normal routine into a life of *yiras Shamayim* and introspection?

I was prompted to write this work as a result of this confusion, which exists even among *bnei Torah*.

I am fully aware of my personal deficiencies and know that I am not worthy of writing about matters concerning *teshuvah* and *yiras Shamayim*. But I am not writing words of reproof. Rather, my goal is to open the gates to those who wish to begin to tread upon the path of *teshuvah* but do not know how.

The words found in this pamphlet are largely based on the accepted works of Mussar.

May Hashem assist me and may this book bring benefit to those who read it.

S. W.
Menachem Av, 5749

Table of Contents

Elul:
The Gateway to Teshuvah

The First Gate

Rosh Chodesh Elul

IF A PERSON does not begin the process of *teshuvah* on the first day of the month of Elul, it is almost certain that he will not ascend in spirituality during the month. It is a well-known phenomenon: one who disregards the signals that are meant to awaken him to *teshuvah* damages his sensitivity to such signals in the future. The first moments of the shofar blowing on Rosh Chodesh Elul are extremely precious; it follows that one must awaken himself to do *teshuvah* immediately. How does one achieve this?

Before we discuss various methods of *teshuvah*, we must first focus on the spiritual situation in which we find ourselves during the year, for it is impossible to specify the remedy to a malady before the malady has been clearly diagnosed; similarly, it is impossible to suggest methods to overcome spiritual maladies without first identifying our spiritual state.

The Second Gate

Man's Daily Actions

IT IS DIFFICULT for an individual to evaluate and assess his actions consistently and thereby conform to all the rules stipulated in the four sections of the *Shulchan Aruch*. This difficulty is felt even by religious people who are fully committed to the Torah.

Consequently, one's actions during the year are determined by his habits, which are ingrained into his personality from childhood. He does not question the righteousness of his acts nor is he aware of the numerous mitzvos that he trespasses from day to day.

This is a brief description of the spiritual state that we find ourselves in today. Now, the shofar says, "Wake up from your sleep! You are blinded by illusions! Things are not right!"

We listen to the sound of the shofar and hear its message, but we are not affected; we do not want to accept the responsibilities that its message implies. We fear that if we reflect upon the quality of our spiritual endeavors, we will have no choice but to change our ways. Therefore, we choose not to ponder over the shofar's message.

The question that must be asked at this point is: How can we begin to repent when we lack the will to do so?

The Third Gate

Strengthening Tefillah and Torah Study

THE PROCESS OF *teshuvah*, which begins on Rosh Chodesh Elul and continues until Yom Kippur, may be successfully achieved if it is performed in a gradual manner.

The First Step

Initially, the areas of *avodah* which are already strong should be further strengthened. They should be reinforced with an added quality of attentiveness: being careful to avoid sin and meticulous in the performance of mitzvos.

Strengthening Tefillah

One should strengthen his *tefillah* by becoming more punctilious about the times of *tefillah*. In addition, one should endeavor to improve the quality of his *tefillah* by increasing his level of concentration and intention. The simple meaning of the words of *Kriyas Shema* and the first blessing of the *She-*

moneh Esrei should be clearly understood. Special emphasis should be put on raising one's level of concentration during the recital of the prayers *Ahavah Rabbah, Atah Chonein Le'adam, Hashiveinu, Selach Lanu,* and the first blessing of *Birkas Hamazon.*

Strengthening Torah Study

Every person should reinforce his Torah study, according to his individual level of scholarly capability. Torah scholars whose sole occupation is the study of Torah should become more punctual and begin the study sessions on time. Extra care should be devoted to avoiding conversations that are irrelevent to Torah study in the *beis midrash.*

Those who are not able to devote their entire day to Torah study should be stricter than ever about studying Torah during the hours they have set aside for this purpose.

Strengthening Tefillah and Torah Study
Uplifts the Person

Strengthening *tefillah* and Torah study is an essential prerequisite to the process of *teshuvah.* Since these things are not new to an individual and his environment reinforces these mitzvos, becoming stronger in these two areas is something that is more easily attained. This has a great impact on a person. In addition, *tefillah* and Torah study spiritually uplift a person and thereby increase his will to repent and correct his ways. As the Sages said, "A mitzvah brings in its wake another mitzvah."[1]

---

1. *Avos* 4:2.

The Fourth Gate

Mussar Study

The Second Step

One should devote a half-hour a day to the study of Mussar. During the first days of Elul, *sefarim* that discuss the strengthening of Torah study should be studied, for example, *Maalos Hatorah*, by the brother of the Vilna Gaon, and the fourth chapter of *Nefesh Hachaim*. One should generally look for methods by which to strengthen Torah study.

The Third Step

After a number of days of consistent Mussar study, one should study *sefarim* that discuss *yiras Shamayim* and *teshuvah* in general, for example, "*Shaar Hateshuvah*," in the *sefer Orchos Tzaddikim*, and the second chapter of *Shaarei Teshuvah* written by Rabbeinu Yonah (especially from *maamar* 10 and onwards).

At this time one should not begin to examine the righteousness of his deeds; this often brings on some degree of melancholy, an emotional state which can erroneously lead one to feel that he is incapable of change and therefore cease the process of *teshuvah. Tefillah* and Torah study should therefore be strengthened for a few more days, before beginning self-examination.

The Fourth Step

Approximately ten days of reinforcement of *tefillah*, Torah, and Mussar are sufficient to prepare one for the next stage of the *teshuvah* process: introspection.

One should ponder over his daily schedule and evaluate whether his actions are in accordance with the rules stipulated in the *Shulchan Aruch*. For example, the individual should reexamine how he acts when he awakens, what he does before *tefillah*, and whether his actions are according to Halachah. He should then write down those behaviors which need reinforcement. Similarly, he should reassess the manner in which he relates to his family, friends, and acquaintances. He should carefully evaluate his manner of speech and tone of voice—are they offensive?—his willingness to perform acts of *chessed*, and whether his actions, in general, need correction.

At this stage, it is unnecessary to decide on specific *methods* of character correction. Rather, the goal of this stage of the *teshuvah* process is to accurately identify those character traits that are deficient.

The Fifth Gate

Elul Resolutions

The Fifth Step

Following the steps described above, one should begin to learn the first chapter of Rabbeinu Yonah's *Shaarei Teshuvah*. One section should be studied daily. This study should begin approximately two weeks after Rosh Chodesh Elul, and the entire chapter should be completed by Yom Kippur. The method of study should be the following: One should review the words many times until their meaning becomes clear. He should continue to review over and over again those points that affect him profoundly, until they penetrate deep into his heart.

How to Make Resolutions

If one should feel an overwhelming desire to accept a resolution upon himself, he should first determine whether it is something that he will be able to accomplish. He should only make resolutions that he feels are within his ability to fulfill. At this point, it is advisable to make only one resolution and keep it only until after Yom Kippur, or even for only one or two weeks. For example, one who has a strong desire to read newspapers or listen to the news should make a resolution to refrain from doing so for a specific period of time.

It is important to stress that if one should fail to fulfill his resolution, he should not become discouraged from continuing on the path to *teshuvah*. Rather, he should realize that human nature renders people susceptible to enticement and that his failure to fulfill his resolution is understandable. He should simply try again. Perhaps the resolution that he made was too stringent for him, in which case he should lighten the conditions of the resolution.

One should be very careful not to make resolutions in Elul that are beyond his capabilities to fulfill. For example, one should not resolve to wake up an hour, or even half an hour, earlier than usual, which is very difficult since it requires a person to condition his body to a different schedule. It is therefore most probable that he will fail in his efforts to fulfill this resolution.

There is not enough time in the month of Elul to fight a head-on battle with one's entire nature. Defeat in such a struggle brings on melancholy, with attendant feelings of desperation and low self-esteem.

The Sixth Gate

Self-Assessment

APPROXIMATELY TEN DAYS before Rosh Hashanah, a more specific self-analysis should be performed. Before we discuss the methodology of self-analysis, the reader should be aware of the following fact: There are two types of transgressions, and each requires a different method of correction.

Irregular Transgressions

There are transgressions that the God-fearing Jew generally avoids. Occasionally, however, for various reasons the *yetzer hara* overpowers him and he sins, either unintentionally, intentionally, or through a mental lapse. The prayers and supplications recited during Elul and Yom Kippur, in combination with a firm decision to refrain from performing such transgressions in the future, will suffice to ensure that such an individual correct his ways. In addition, sincere feelings of regret over transgressions committed in the past will guard against the commission of transgressions in the future.

The list of areas of weakness that require reinforcement (see step four) should be studied regularly during the year for the purpose of maintaining the level of self-awareness reached during Elul.

Such irregular transgressions include: tardiness in *tefillah*; vulgar speech; reading material that stimulates one's desires; consumption of foods that are not under reliable rabbinic supervision; embarrassing people in public; talking during the reading of the Torah or Kaddish; etc.

When thinking of transgressions that involved one's desires, the individual should not picture in his mind the exact details of his transgression. By the same token, one should not ponder over what could have happened had he not controlled himself and refrained from transgressing, since these types of thoughts are not only unhelpful, but are also harmful.

It is a well-known axiom that a person is where his thoughts are. Thinking about past sins, in effect, repeats the sins. This is analogous to one who cleans out his trash can. Even though his intentions are to rid himself of the trash, his hands nonetheless become dirty.

Habitual Transgressions

Various factors combine to cause a person to sin regularly, both in accidental and intentional sins. For example, lack of attention and lack of knowledge of Halachah can cause one to unknowingly commit daily transgressions.

Such habitual transgressions include: *lashon hara*; frivolity; a lack of intention during the recital of *tefillah* and blessings; uttering the name of Hashem in vain; repeated tardiness in *tefillah*; discussing non-Torah topics during hours appointed for Torah study; lack of control over one's eyes; anger, pride, jealousy, baseless hatred; performing prohibited *melachos* during

Chol Hamoed and Yom Tov; fraud, dishonesty; glee over others' tribulations; lack of respect for one's parents; and lack of respect for Torah scholars, teachers, and older people. And neglecting Torah study outweighs them all.

Correction of the many transgressions and undesirable character traits enumerated above cannot be achieved at once. Human nature can only be changed gradually, in small increments, a process that may take years, and not by sporadic and haphazard attempts to tackle all of one's deficiencies at one time. The goal of the month of Elul should not be to correct one's character traits. Instead, during Elul one should strive to make a decision to begin on a methodical process of character correction. This will, in fact, somewhat mitigate the individual's past transgressions; his decision to correct himself demonstrates that his past sins were due to a lack of awareness and not intentional.

Man has many corrupt characteristics, which cause him to desire honor, wealth, and the satisfaction of basic desires. When the age of Bar Mitzvah is attained, these desires must be tempered and controlled despite the inherent difficulties in doing so. In general, a Bar Mitzvah boy is not capable of achieving such control over his desires. What then, does He expect us to do? How can we be expected to overcome human nature? The Sages have taught that Hashem does not have unreasonable expectations for His creation!

The answer is that we are expected to strive to slowly correct our faults through constant effort. Through a methodical process of *teshuvah*, we hope to eventually correct ourselves. The only accusation that one may be charged with is "You did not try hard enough!" If one tries to overcome his faults to the best of his abilities, Hashem will help him achieve his goal. As the Sages said, "If it were not that Hashem helps a person overcome his *yetzer hara,* he would not succeed."[1]

One should not be discouraged by failure. Even though success may not be apparent, one must have faith that his efforts were not in vain. In the Next World, the individual will be handsomely rewarded for every bit of effort he expended in order to correct himself, as "the reward is commensurate with the exertion."[2]

Whoever follows these directions will certainly succeed in his aspirations to do *teshuvah.*

---

1. *Kiddushin* 30b.
2. *Avos* 5:26.

The Seventh Gate

Words of Encouragement

OUR SAGES SAY that just as people's faces differ, so, too, their spiritual makeups. Since every person is unique, some people will succeed where others fail. One should, therefore, not become disheartened at another person's success. One person may face difficult tests; another's challenges may be much easier.

A person may put in honest toil and still feel unsuccessful, as if he has not progressed at all. Should one feel that failure has befallen him, he may be comforted by the following metaphor: Once, a ship sank close to shore. The passengers tried with all their strength to reach the safety of dry land. Despite slow progress, they continued swimming. What drove them on was the knowledge that each stroke brought them closer to safety. When, at long last, the shore came into sight, the difficulty of their situation became altogether alleviated. Their strength increased the moment the promise of safety could be perceived by their senses. However, if they had been swimming on a dark night and not seen the shore, they would have continued in painful uncertainty. A person who truly values his life does not become discouraged because he cannot see the shore. The knowledge that each stroke is bringing him closer to safety is enough to motivate him to continue his painful progress. Once the journey is over, and he walks on terra firma, the pain of his self-rescue is quickly forgotten.

This is also true of the person who embarks on the journey to *avodas Hashem*. He should not become distracted by lack of achievement. He must understand that every bit of effort he expends to reach perfection brings him one step closer to his goal. Even when he still feels entrapped by the *yetzer hara*, he must concentrate on going forward and reassure himself that every step is bringing him closer to freedom. Eventually, he, too, will see the shore on the horizon.

The Eighth Gate

Assessing One's Deeds

THIS CHAPTER WILL describe the method by which to correct the transgressions and undesirable character traits of the habitual transgressor.

One should make a list of those areas he feels need reinforcement. One of the character traits or habitual transgressions which the individual feels strongly about should then be selected, and a resolution made concerning it. People who make more than one resolution generally fail; it is, therefore, advisable to make a single resolution that can be fulfilled rather than several that cannot.

For example, one who habitually arrives at shul late should resolve to arrive two minutes before the *tefillah*. (Here is a simple way to convince oneself of the importance of arriving punctually at shul: The *Shulchan Aruch* states that *Pesukei Dezimrah* must be recited before the *tefillah*. One must also allow time for putting on his *tallis* and *tefillin* and for the prayers before *Baruch Sheamar*. It is necessary, therefore, to arrive a few minutes before *tefillah*.) Similarly, a person who regularly accepts Shabbos at the last minute should resolve to ready himself for Shabbos ten minutes before the appointed time.

Each individual must determine what resolution would be most beneficial for his particular needs. For example, one person may decide to try to fulfill the obligation to say *Hamapil* and *Kriyas Shema* before sleep more punctiliously, while another may resolve to remember to wash his hands next to his bed in the morning or say *Amen* and *Yehei Shemei Rabbah* with greater concentration.

What about the other transgressions on the list? As we noted earlier, the sincere intention to begin to strive methodically to correct oneself suffices for the moment. Naturally, during the Holy Days one wishes to build a platform from which he may begin to wage war against the *yetzer hara*. One must speculate and determine what causes him to sin, what is the root of his problem. The following verse from Iyov (28:28) prescribes the method: "And to man He said, 'Behold, the fear of the Lord is wisdom, and to depart from evil is understanding.' "

Let us take an account of our transgressions: As we wrote in "the second gate," much of our *avodah* is habitual and superficial. During the year, we recite thousands of *berachos* without concentrating. We wash our hands before eating bread mindlessly, out of habit. We ready ourselves physically for Shabbos, but we refrain from preparing ourselves spiritually. Except for *tefillah*, we are very far removed from *yiras Hashem* during our daily rounds. The first halachah in the *Shulchan Aruch* is the obligation to be constantly aware of Hashem's existence. The inability to fulfill this obligation is a major cause of our other transgressions.

It was noted above that one of our major problems is

lack of intention during *tefillah* and *berachos*. In truth, this is only a symptom of the real disease, the root of which is the inability to perceive Hashem's existence. The appropriate cure for this problem is to come closer to Hashem. If one is successful in achieving a greater awareness of this concept the disease will cure itself and subsequently the symptoms will become alleviated. However, if one does not incorporate this concept into his awareness, the same symptoms will plague the individual for the rest of his life. The resolutions described above will only be effective in alleviating symptoms if the root of the disease is treated at the same time.

The prescribed cure for the disease is to increase our level of *yiras Shamayim*.[1] How do we accomplish this? The basis of *yiras Shamayim* is the realization that there is a Creator. An individual's *yiras Shamayim* will increase according to the degree that he internalizes this realization. One can internalize the realization that there is a Creator by pondering the basic components of *emunah*: that the Creator is all-powerful and all-encompassing; that He reigns over the entire world and each one of its inhabitants; that He is aware of our actions and perceives our innermost thoughts and feelings; and that He rewards those who fulfill His precepts and punishes those who violate them. Reciting the *Ani Maamin* is an effective way to review these concepts.

With constant reviewing of these concepts, the realization that there is a Creator will gradually become more and more internalized, which is one of the important tasks that must be accomplished during the month of Elul.

---

1. *Shaarei Teshuvah*, ch. 1, letter 11.

The Ninth Gate

The Correction of Character Traits

THE PREVIOUS CHAPTERS have mentioned the difficulty of curbing desires and correcting specific failings in a short time. We will now discuss some general methods to help the individual with character correction.

One must understand and believe that negative character traits are truly harmful to the individual. The more sensitive one becomes to the unfavorable consequences of a trait, the closer he is to correcting it. One must come to the realization that the negative character trait is ultimately destructive to him. For example, a person who is easily angered lives a life of strain and emotional stress. A person who feels undue pride is ridiculed by his peers. A jealous person never experiences prolonged periods of satisfaction.

Whoever ponders these concepts will conclude that those character traits that distract people from treading the true path are made of vanity and emptiness. The most effective weapon against this enemy is logic and common sense, and that is the meaning of the verse: "And to man He said, 'Behold, the fear of the Lord is wisdom, and to depart from evil is understanding'" (Iyov 28:28). One must approach one's negative character traits with wisdom and look for their source in order to uproot them.

The Tenth Gate

Distancing Oneself from Desire

THE MOST IMPORTANT rule to distance oneself from desire is to avoid situations that may negatively arouse one's senses. Once the senses are aroused, the *yetzer hara* gains a foothold in the heart. Then, even an individual who considers himself to have *yiras Shamayim* is in great danger of failure. The *yetzer hara* is a master of deception and confusion. It will convince you that an act that will satisfy your desire is totally permitted. At this point, the ability to reason will be seriously hampered. The most effective way to control desire is to completely avoid temptation. Controlling the eyes is the first step towards avoiding temptation.

One should meditate that there is nothing to gain from fulfilling desires. As one of the *Rishonim* said, "Know that desire is not advantageous to the individual. Rather, it causes embarrassment and unhappiness."

Conclusion

THE VARIOUS METHODS of *teshuvah* described above were written with an emphasis for application during the month of Elul. Elul is such an emotionally and spiritually charged month that I thought it appropriate to provide a spirtiual "first aid" kit which would enable the reader to achieve the goals that characterize it.

In truth, the essential method by which one may ascend spiritually is the constant study of *sifrei yirah,* which increases awareness of *yiras Hashem* and the importance of the mitz-vos. For example, one who habitually speaks *lashon hara* and wishes to stop has no alternative other than to begin an intensive study of the halachos regarding *lashon hara* and the ethical ramifications of transgressing this prohibition. Both are discussed at length in the *sefarim* of the Chafetz Chaim. Similarly, the remedy for one who finds it difficult to daven in the prescribed times is to study those sections of the *Shulchan Aruch* or *Mishnah Berurah* that discuss the subject.

R. Yisrael Salanter, *zt"l*, of blessed memory, was of the opinion that the study of Halachah causes a person to re-evaluate the importance of the subject being discussed, which, in turn, stimulates the person to fulfill the mitzvos with greater devotion.

The correction of character traits demands prolonged study of works that discuss negative traits. For example, the *Orchos Tzaddikim*, *Mesilas Yesharim*, and the Rambam's *Hil-chos De'os* and *Hilchos Teshuvah* will bring about a reevalua-tion of one's character traits. The traits that the individual considered to be in order before embarking on this program of study may well become newly defined as derogatory. This realization is the first step towards true character correction, which, hopefully, will then become a reality.

The Mussar *sefarim* describe man's spiritual *avodah* in this world as a long battle that does not allow for swift defeat of the enemy. The battle against the *yetzer hara* is eternal. Despite mortal man's inherent weaknesses such as forgetful-ness and distraction, which cause him to stumble time after time, one must continue the battle at all costs.

To help wage this battle against the *yetzer hara*, Hashem gave man Yom Kippur. It is a day during which we are purified from our sins, a day that strengthens us and enables us to achieve our life's purpose—to come close to Hashem for eternity. We begin the new year with vigor and strength, determined to increase the quality of our *avodah*.

The Practical Guide to Teshuvah

Introduction

R. YISRAEL SALANTER, *zt"l*, wrote that the most difficult task of *teshuvah* on Yom Kippur is to resolve to refrain from continuing to violate a specific mitzvah.[1] R. Itzaleh Peterburger, *zt"l*, explains that this difficulty stems from our confusing prohibitions with permitted actions. We make this mistake because of our consistent and habitual repetition of the prohibited actions.[2] Similarly, the Gemara says that a person who repeatedly transgresses a mitzvah will eventually come to think that his sin is, in fact, permitted.[3] In addition, R. Itzaleh wrote that we lack recognition of the true severity of our transgressions and their stringent ramifications and punishments. We also do not fully comprehend the sanctity of Hashem.

---

1. *Ohr Yisrael*, letter 15.

2. *Kochvei Ohr*, ch. 7.

3. *Kiddushin* 20b.

Despite these drawbacks, we do know the Torah is eternal and even our generation is expected to do *teshuvah*. Indeed, a guarantee of our success is written in the Torah. As it says, "When you are in distress and all these things come upon you, in the latter days, if you turn to Hashem, your God, and hear his voice...He will not forsake you nor destroy you..." (Devarim 4:30-31). As Rabbeinu Yonah points out, the Torah also states that Hashem will help those who strive to do *teshuvah*, even if their character traits impair their ability to achieve this goal.[4] As it says, "And Hashem, your God, will circumcise your heart...that you may live" (Devarim 30:6).

For this reason, I present this collection of insights from various *teshuvah sefarim*. Following are some of the *sefarim* from which this collection was drawn: *Chovos Halevavos, Beis Elokim* written by the Mabit, *Orchos Tzaddikim, Nesiv Hateshuvah* written by the Maharal, *Shaarei Teshuvah* written by Rabbeinu Yonah, and *Hilchos Teshuvah* written by the Rambam.

I have added explanations to this manuscript that will, with the help of Hashem, shed light on some of the topics discussed.

May it be the will of Hashem that the verse be fulfilled: "And [you] shall return to Hashem, your God, and hear His voice...And Hashem, your God, will overturn your captivity and have compassion on you, and will return and gather you from all the nations among whom Hashem, your God, has scattered you" (Devarim 30:2-3).

And may we be spared the tribulations of the days of the Mashiach.

S. W.
22 Menachem Av, 5750.

---

4. *Shaarei Teshuvah*, ch. 1, letter 1.

Chapter One

The Value of Teshuvah

A Selection of Statements from the Rambam's Hilchos Teshuvah

1) The value of *teshuvah* is indeed great, for it causes man to come close to the Shechinah, as it says, "Come back, O Israel, to Hashem your God" [Hoshea 14:2].

Yesterday, this disdained and detested man was hated by Hashem. Today, he is loved and regarded favorably. Yesterday, this man was alienated from Hashem, the God of Israel, as it says, "Your sins will separate you from your God" [Yeshayah 59:2]. He pleaded for help, but no one heeded his call. He did mitzvos, only to have them flung back at him. Today, he is attached to the Shechinah. His pleas for help are answered immediately. His mitzvos are accepted gracefully and joyously. As it says, "Your God has already accepted your deeds" [Koheles 9:2].[1]

---

1. Ch. 7, halachah 7.

2) A *baal teshuvah* should not feel that his spiritual level is lower than that of *tzaddikim*, for this is false! Rather, he is loved and adored by Hashem as if he had never sinned before.[2]

3) *Teshuvah* atones for all transgressions. A person who committed transgressions throughout his lifetime, and then did *teshuvah*, will not be reminded of his transgressions in the Next World.[3]

4) One who dies in a state of *teshuvah* merits to have all of his transgressions forgiven.[4]

Selections from Midrashim

1) One who claims Hashem does not accept the *teshuvah* of *baalei teshuvah* should be refuted in the following manner: King Menashe, who committed more sins than anyone ever did, was totally pardoned for all his sins when he did *teshuvah*. As it says, "And Hashem granted his request, and He accepted his prayer" [Divrei Hayamim II 33:13].[5]

2) "It is good to admit one's wrongs to Hashem." This was uttered by Adam Harishon to teach generations to come that anyone who acknowledges his guilt over having sinned, and subsequently refrains from continuing to do so, will be saved from the purgatory of Gehenom.[6]

Selections from Sifrei Kadmonim

1) The verse says "...Hashem, Hashem..." [Shemos 34:6]. The Sages interpreted this verse to mean that Hashem says,

---

2. Ibid., halachah 4.
3. Ch. 1, halachah 3.
4. Ch. 2, halachah 1.
5. *Midrash Rabbah*, Bemidbar 14:4.
6. *Midrash Shachar Tov*, Tehillim 92:2.

"I am Hashem before man sins, and I am Hashem after man sins and subsequently does *teshuvah*."[7] The Beis Elokim explains that when a sinner does *teshuvah*, Hashem cleanses him of his sins. Consequently, that person becomes as dear to Hashem as he was before he committed those sins. This is the meaning of "I am Hashem before man sins, and I am Hashem after man sins...." Just as man was dear to Hashem before he sinned, so too after he does *teshuvah* is he loved.[8]

2) It is written in the Torah that Hashem will help those who yearn to do *teshuvah* but lack the attributes to achieve this goal. He will reinvigorate their souls with purity, as it says, "And you will repent to Hashem your God, and you will hearken to His voice" [Devarim 30:2]. Another verse says, "And Hashem will circumcise your heart and the heart of your offspring" [Devarim 30:6].[9]

3) The moment he repents, the sinner is considered to be a *tzaddik*. This is true despite the fact that Yom Kippur has not passed, and he has not suffered any punishments for his past transgressions yet. This is proven by the following statement: "A man who says to a woman, 'You are now married to me on the condition that I am a *tzaddik*,' is considered to be legally married.[10] This is true even if the man was a sworn sinner. The reason is it is possible that he had feelings of repentance in his heart.[11]

4) *Teshuvah* protects the penitent from tribulations. Beginning with the initial stages of *teshuvah*, Hashem protects the *baal teshuvah* from suffering and harmful circumstances that were decreed as a result of his sins. As it says, "...Shalom,

7. *Rosh Hashanah* 17b.

8. "*Shaar Hateshuvah*," ch. 1.

9. *Shaarei Teshuvah*, ch. 1, letter 1.

10. *Kiddushin* 49b.

11. *Beis Elokim*, "*Shaar Hateshuvah*," ch. 2.

Shalom, to the far and to the near" [Yeshayah 57:19]. "Shalom" refers to the penitent, who will feel at ease and tranquil about the effects of his past sins. Since *teshuvah* delays retribution and Yom Kippur atones for sin, this applies even if he violated negative precepts specified in the Torah. *Teshuvah* suspends judgement, thereby protecting the penitent from the forces of retribution, while Yom Kippur takes the place of the punishment.[12]

---

12. Ibid., chs. 1-2.

Chapter Two

The Definition of Teshuvah

THIS CHAPTER WILL be devoted to defining the meaning of the term "*teshuvah*." Later chapters will discuss different methods through which one can come to do *teshuvah*.

The term "*teshuvah*" has two meanings:

1) To return to one's original place of departure. This meaning appears in the verse, "*Vayashav Avraham el ne'arav...*"— "And Avraham returned to his attendants..." (Bereishis 22:19).

2) To distance oneself from a certain location or situation. This meaning appears in the verse, "*Shuv mecharon apecha*"—"Abandon Your anger" (Shemos 32:12). Moshe Rabbeinu beseeched Hashem to distance Himself from His anger and rage. Similarly, this is the meaning of the verse, "He continuously withholds His anger" (Tehillim 78:38).

Both meanings appear in the works of the Sages.

The Rambam[1] writes that the mitzvah of *teshuvah* is fulfilled by disassociating oneself from sin. This definition is similar to the second definition. The Beis Elokim writes that the mitzvah of *teshuvah* is fulfilled by discontinuing past actions.[2] However, he writes that the essential meaning of the term "*teshuvah*" is to come close to Hashem, which can be achieved by distancing oneself from sin.[3]

The Chovos Halevavos writes that the word "*teshuvah*" implies the individual must correct himself to the degree that he becomes, once again, suitable to undertake *avodas Hashem*. Since sin rendered him unsuitable for *avodas Hashem*, *teshuvah* is achieved when he successfully reinstates the spiritual state he was in before he sinned.[4]

The Maharal writes that the essential meaning of the term "*teshuvah*" is that the transgressor returns to Hashem.[5] The source for this meaning of the word is the verse, "Shalom, Shalom to the far and to the near" (Yeshayah 57:19). Shalom to the one who is far away, and shalom to the one who has become close through *teshuvah*. One who has sinned and not done *teshuvah* has become distanced from Hashem. This concept is analogous to a subject who stands in the presence of his king. He would not dare transgress the king's decree in his presence. He would only dare rebel against the king's doctrines when he has distanced himself from the king. Since Hashem's glory fills the entire world, we only dare to sin when we fail to perceive His existence. Conversely, a sinner's repentance is, in effect, an acknowledgement that Hashem sees his actions. The penitent thus comes to

---

1. *Hilchos Teshuvah*, ch. 2, halachah 2.

2. "*Shaar Hateshuvah*," ch. 2.

3. Ibid., ch. 1.

4. "*Shaar Hateshuvah*," ch.1.

5. *Nesiv Hateshuvah*, end of ch. 3.

the realization that Hashem is close to him.

This is the meaning of the verse, "Repent, O Israel, to Hashem your God" (Hoshea 14:2). In other words, return from the place to which you have banished yourself and be, once again, close to Him. *Teshuvah* gradually causes an individual to come so close to Hashem that he eventually feels he is standing before the *Kisei Hakavod*. As the Sages have said, "Great is *teshuvah*, for it reaches the *Kisei Hakavod*."[6] From this statement, we learn that one should do *teshuvah* until he is able to imagine that he is in the presence of the *Kisei Hakavod*.[7] Let us further explain the two aspects of *teshuvah* defined above and their ramifications:

1) To come close to Hashem. This is analogous to a rebellious son who leaves home to follow his heart's desire. After some time, he begins to reminisce about the good treatment he received from his father. Memories of his father's love cause him to regret his rebellious acts, which in turn awakens a great urge in him to return home and ask for forgiveness. When he returns home, to his great distress, the son discovers that his father is absent. What does he do? He begins to search for his father, asking everyone where he is. Finally, after great effort, he finds him. He manages to call out through his tears, "Father, Father!"

Similarly, transgressors will feel empty and despondent. Unable to find contentment, they will eventually return to their Creator and do *teshuvah*. To return, they must fulfill the requirement to call out to Hashem for help. As the verse says, "If from there you search for Hashem, your God, you will find Him, if you seek Him with all your heart and with all your soul" (Devarim 4:29). The degree of closeness achieved by this *teshuvah* is proportional to the intensity of the call for help.

---

6. *Yoma* 86a.

7. *Beis Elokim*, "*Shaar Hateshuvah*," ch. 1.

This is the primary *avodah* of the month of Elul—to come close to Hashem. This is similar to the statement of the Chovos Halevavos that the meaning of the word "*teshuvah*" is "that the individual must correct himself to the degree that he becomes once again suitable to undertake *avodas Hashem*," which is certainly the initial stage of the process of *teshuvah*.

2) To uproot the sin. Constant introspection and reflection on methods that will prevent oneself from repeating the sin uproot sin. This is analogous to one who finds himself in a place infested by mosquitoes and bees. He must first escape. Once he has escaped, he may easily rid himself of the few insects that have followed him. Still, he will have to experience the pain of the insect bites. The meaning of this analogy is easily understood.

Chapter Three

"It is entirely up to me!"

THE *RISHONIM* LIST various circumstances that motivate a person to do *teshuvah*: tribulations, rebuke, old age, the ten days of *teshuvah*, and so on. In truth, the essential urge to do *teshuvah* must emanate from one's will. As the Rambam explains, *teshuvah* is an expression of free will.[1] Hillel said, "If I am not for myself, who will be for me?"[2] One should realize that no one can do *teshuvah* for him, neither his parents, friends, or teachers, not a *tzaddik*, nor a rebbe, nor an angel.

It is entirely up to me!

This concept is discussed in tractate *Avodah Zarah*.[3] The Gemara tells the following story:

Elazar Ben Durdaya transgressed every mitzvah in the Torah. He eventually felt remorse over his transgressions

---

1. *Hilchos Teshuvah*, beg. of ch. 5.

2. *Avos* 1:14.

3. 17a.

and wanted to do *teshuvah*. He was told that his *teshuvah* would not be accepted, so he went to the mountains and cried out, "Ask for my forgiveness!" His plea was to no avail. He cried out, "Heavens and Earth, ask for my forgiveness!"—to no avail. He cried out to the sun and the moon, the stars and the constellations, all to no avail. He then came to the realization that the decision to do *teshuvah* depended only on his own will. "It is entirely up to me!"

He bent his head between his knees and began to weep so violently that his soul left him. A *bas kol* announced, "Rebbi Elazar Ben Durdaya has acquired a place in the Next World."

Truly—"It is entirely up to me."

Chapter Four

The Elements of Teshuvah

THE *RISHONIM* ENUMERATED the four elements of *te-shuvah*:

1. Regret
2. Forsaking sin
3. Confession and the request for forgiveness
4. Resolve to refrain from sin

These four components of *teshuvah* appear in the *seder havidui* (confession recitation) of Yom Kippur. Regret is expressed in the words, "Here I am before You like a utensil filled with shame." Forsaking sin and resolve to refrain from sin in the future are expressed in the words, "May it be Your will [to assist me] that I should not sin again." Confession and the request for forgiveness are expressed in the words, "And for all these, God of forgiveness, forgive us, pardon us, cleanse us."

The Chovos Halevavos writes that atonement can only

be attained by implementing all four elements.[1] This concept is also implied by the Rambam, who states that a sinner can even do *teshuvah* on the last day of his life.[2] The Rambam then asks, "What is *teshuvah*? It is when the sinner refrains from continuing to sin and resolves to refrain from committing the transgression in the future. He must also feel regret over his past actions, confess his past sins, and vocalize the resolve to refrain from committing sins in the future."

Most important, the Rambam writes, "The words 'But rather we have sinned' are the essential component of confession."[3] In other words, even though the penitent should include remorse and the resolve to refrain from future sin in his confession, failure to do so will not detract from the validity of his confession, for uttering the words "But rather we have sinned" is the essence of confession.

The Beis Elokim's opinion is that a sinner is considered to be a *tzaddik* if he merely forsakes sin and feels remorse over past transgressions; these two components alone are a complete *teshuvah*. His proof for this contention is that the meaning of the word "*teshuvah*" is to distance oneself from sin, which includes the forsaking of sin and feelings of remorse over past transgressions. According to the Beis Elokim, the other elements of *teshuvah* are meant to strengthen the two essential elements. Confession and the resolve to refrain from sin in the future cause the sinner to feel humility and shame.[4]

One who attains all of the components of *teshuvah* outlined in *Shaarei Teshuvah* and *Chovos Halevavos*[5] is considered

---

1. "*Shaar Hateshuvah*," ch. 4.

2. *Hilchos Teshuvah*, ch. 2, halachah 2.

3. Ibid., halachah 8, and see *Lechem Mishnah*.

4. *Beis Elokim*, "*Shaar Hateshuvah*," ch. 3.

5. "*Shaar Hateshuvah*," ch. 5.

to be a *baal teshuvah*, literally, a "master of *teshuvah*" which means that he has achieved complete *teshuvah*. This is the ultimate level of *teshuvah*. Such a penitent is guaranteed that he will not commit the same sin again.

The statement by the Sages that a *baal teshuvah* reaches a level that a *tzaddik* cannot reach[6] refers to an exalted level of *teshuvah*, which is accomplished by performing all the requirements of *teshuvah* and, in addition, coming close to Hashem in the following ways: sadness, distress, and anxiety over sins, humbleness, the forsaking of sin, the correction of character traits, controlling one's desires, prayer, requesting forgiveness, and repeated confession of sins through the last day of life. Such an individual is greater than a *tzaddik* who never sinned, since "the reward is proportional to the effort expended" (see chapter 20). But the *teshuvah* of one who returned and sinned after repentance is not annulled; his sin is reckoned as a wholly new one.[7]

---

6. *Berachos* 34b.
7. *Beis Elokim*, "*Shaar Hateshuvah*," ch. 3. See also chs. 16-17.

Chapter Five

Regret

REGRET OVER PAST transgressions has the effect of retroactively uprooting one's sins. One may wonder how it is possible to correct an apparently irreversible fact. How can a man who killed another possibly make amends for his act? The answer is Hashem, in His great mercy, saw fit to decree that a deed is considered nullified if the desire to do it is nullified. This is similar to the halachos concerning *nedarim* (vows) stipulating that the *neder* may be annulled if the vower feels remorse over it.

It says, "...and your iniquity is taken away, and your sin is purged" (Yeshayah 6:7). This verse implies that sin can be completely uprooted, even to the extent that it will be regarded as if it never existed at all.[1]

The Maharal offers a different explanation of why *teshu-*

---

1. *Mesilas Yesharim*, end of ch. 4.

vah uproots sin retroactively.[2] Man is composed of both a physical self and a spiritual self. His physical nature imposes certain demands on him, such as the need for food, water, and the like. Due to these physical demands, man cannot be a purely spiritual and intellectual being. According to the Sages, "a person only sins when foolishness overtakes him,"[3] i.e., the spiritual self never fully participates in the performance of a sin and, therefore, remains primarily pure. The main part of man that does *teshuvah* is the spiritual self. The act of *teshuvah* reaffirms that his spiritual self never fully participates in the transgression, and this reaffirmation, in turn, causes the sin to become uprooted. Conversely, a sinner who refrains from doing *teshuvah* reveals in effect that even his spiritual self did fully participate in the performance of the transgression.

Regret Must Be Vocalized

The *Rishonim* are of the opinion that regret must be articulated. For example, the Rambam writes that recitation of confession should include the following words: "I regret and am embarrassed over my past actions."[4] The Chovos Halevavos explains that regret must be expressed verbally because *teshuvah* is similar to relations between men: When one man harms another, it is easier for the harmed person to forgive him when he apologizes, so Hashem also pardons the sinner when he voices feelings of regret.[5]

In addition, voicing regret causes the penitent to feel shame, which is the essential component of *teshuvah*. As the Sages say, "One who transgresses and subsequently feels

---

2. *Nesiv Hateshuvah*, ch. 1.

3. *Sotah* 3a.

4. *Hilchos Teshuvah*, ch. 1, halachah 1.

5. "*Shaar Hateshuvah*", ch. 4.

shame is forgiven all his past sins."[6] The fact that the sinner experiences shame demonstrates that he has disassociated himself from sin.[7]

The Beis Elokim adds that voicing feelings of regret will cause the penitent's *teshuvah* to endure.[8]

To Mourn Over Sin

Regret includes lifelong thought and mourning over sins one has committed.[9] The Midrash relates that On (similar to *onan*, a mourner) Ben Peles was so named because for all his life he mourned his intention to join Korach's rebellion against Moshe Rabbeinu.[10] This does not mean that one should allow himself to fall into a state of melancholy; we know that a person should perform God's service with joy. It means that during *tefillah*, or similar times, one should ask for forgiveness for his past sins.

---

6. *Berachos* 12a.

7. *Nesiv Hateshuvah*, ch. 4.

8. "*Shaar Hateshuvah*," ch. 3.

9. *Sefer Hayashar*, Rabbeinu Tam, ch. 10.

10. *Bemidbar Rabbah* 18:20.

Chapter Six

Approaching Teshuvah—I

IT IS CUSTOMARY TO study the Rambam's *Hilchos Teshuvah* and Rabbeinu Yonah's *Shaarei Teshuvah* during the month of Elul. It would be advisable, however, to devote some time and thought to an essential question before studying these texts: What transgressions have I committed? Obviously, before this question has been answered in a specific and clear manner, one cannot hope to feel regret over past sins and do complete *teshuvah*.

The Chovos Halevavos writes that *teshuvah* cannot be achieved unless the penitent comes to realize the unfavorable effects of his actions.[1] Otherwise, he will not be able to feel regret or ask for forgiveness in a sincere manner. This is the meaning of the verse, "I acknowledge my transgressions, and my sin is ever before me" (Tehillim 51:5).

But defining one's sins alone does not guarantee complete

---

1. *"Shaar Hateshuvah,"* ch. 3.

teshuva. Once a person has precisely defined his sins, there is a danger he will become paralyzed by the apparently insurmountable challenge facing him. He may say to himself, "I know myself. I don't have a strong will. It is simply impossible for me to change my ways."

This response occurs as a result of the penitent's ignorance of how to rise to the challenge. One must realize that there are two steps that precede *teshuvah*:

1. To examine at length the severe ramifications of the sin and consider the fact that one is obligated to change his ways.

2. To strengthen oneself through the study of the writings of the Sages concerning the great obligation to do *teshuvah* and review the basic principles of faith, such as reward and punishment and the Great Day of Judgement.[2]

This method will reinforce the penitent's resolve and intensify his desire to distance himself from sin.

The penitent should be aware that, despite all his efforts, it is ultimately impossible to do *teshuvah* without Hashem's help—the *yetzer hara*, is a most fierce enemy. As the Sages say, "Were it not that Hashem helps the penitent to do *teshuvah*, he would not succeed."[3] Obviously, if the penitent does not exert the necessary effort, he cannot expect to receive Divine support. If he does, Hashem saves him from the fangs of the *yetzer hara*, as it says, "The *rasha* (i.e., the *yetzer hara*) awaits to slay the *tzaddik*; Hashem does not abandon him" (Tehillim 37:32).[4]

The Rambam defines the nature of the help Hashem extends to the penitent.[5] One form of this Divine assistance

---

2. See *Shaarei Teshuvah*, ch. 1, letters 10, 12, 16.

3. *Kiddushin* 30b.

4. *Mesilas Yesharim*, end of ch. 2.

5. *Hilchos Teshuvah*, ch. 6, halachah 5.

is His sending the prophets to the Jewish People to inspire them to do *teshuvah*, which is implied by the verse, "Hashem is gracious and caring, for He points out sins" (Tehillim 25:8). This verse refers to the prophets.

In addition, the Rambam writes that Hashem helps one to achieve his spiritual potential by implanting into human nature the ability to learn and understand. This trait was given to each and every person: whoever learns Torah desires to learn more, to achieve greater wisdom and insight. And once on the proper path of spiritual attainment, he naturally strives for even greater achievement. This is the intention of the Sages' statement, "One who desires to become pure receives Divine assistance."[6]

The availability of *sifrei yirah* and the opportunity to study them is the Divine assistance we receive, since it will inspire the penitent to do *teshuvah*.

---

6. *Yoma* 38b.

Chapter Seven

Approaching Teshuvah—II

The First Step Towards Teshuvah

As was discussed in chapter 6, the first step in achieving *teshuvah* is to recognize and define one's sins. There are two general categories of transgressions:

1. Intentional sins, which are committed with full awareness that they are prohibited.

2. Unintentional sins, which are committed from habit. This category can be divided into two types: a) unintentional sins that the penitent would recognize as prohibited if he examined his actions, and b) unintentional sins that the penitent would confuse as permitted even after he examined his actions. (See chapter 12).

Because we violate many prohibitions daily, it is impossible to make an accurate personal accounting unless the transgressions are listed. The following list of transgressions, which appears in the *Orchos Tzaddikim*,[1] will give the reader an idea of some of the sins for which he can do *teshuvah*: Excessive humor and jest, looking at women for the sake of pleasure or to arouse oneself, speaking to women unnecessarily, reciting *tefillah* with little intention (every person according to his level of understanding), speaking in shul, empty-headed frivolity, speaking rudely to others or to poor people (even to one's friends or to people who are on a lower level than him), and worst of all, not studying Torah during the hours set aside for this purpose (*bitul Torah*). In addition, we are guilty of jealousy, baseless hatred, *lashon hara*, pride, and anger. We are not meticulous enough in washing our hands before eating bread or upon arising in the morning, in avoiding damaging people's possessions, and in keeping Shabbos.

When he has completed the list of transgressions which he has committed, the penitent should select a limited number of sins that he feels he can realistically correct within a short span of time. The sins that he selects will often be those that he is capable of avoiding during the year. (See "gates" 6 and 8)

---

1. *"Shaar Hateshuvah."*

Chapter Eight

Approaching Teshuvah—III

The Second Step:
Strengthening the Heart Through Mussar

A person who falls into a state of melancholy because of guilt over past transgressions is regarded as a fool.[1] The penitent should strive to strengthen his resolve to do *teshuvah* and meet the challenge with vigor, vitality, and assertiveness. As the verse says, "Hashem has created a pure heart for me, and He has revitalized my spirits within me" (Tehillim 51:12). Unless the penitent attains these traits and strives with all his might to achieve his goal, his *teshuvah* will not endure. He may develop this aggresive attitude by meditating on these two principles:

1. The great value of mitzvos and the responsibility that is placed on each individual to fulfill them.

2. Failure to reach perfection is the greatest evil.

---

1. *Divrei Torah.*

Contemplation of these two principles will enable the penitent to strive to be counted amongst those who fulfill the precepts of the Torah, which in turn necessitates that he do *teshuvah* and beseech Hashem to forgive his past sins. It is advisable to study the *Shaarei Teshuvah*, especially the first, third, fifth, and seventh chapters. This study, in combination with constant review of these two principles, will enable the penitent to be successful in his striving to do *teshuvah*.

Mussar Study Program

Regular Mussar study sessions are commendable, especially when one plans ahead and determines what material he intends to study during the month of Elul. Unfortunately, lack of planning not only hampers achievement, but may even result in the penitent becoming discouraged and dejected over his lack of progress.

It is, therefore, advisable to plan a program of study at the beginning of every month or every week. During the month of Elul, and until Yom Kippur, Mussar study sessions should be devoted to the study of Rabbeinu Yonah's *Shaarei Teshuvah*, the Rambam's *Hilchos Teshuvah*, and "*Shaar Hateshuvah*" in the *sefer Orchos Tzaddikim*, with each person reviewing the sections he finds particularly applicable or moving.

Chapter Nine

Reinforcement of
Yirah, Teshuvah, and Diligence

THE FOLLOWING SELECTIONS from various sources can serve to strengthen *yiras Shamayim*:

- "...He fills the entire earth with His glory" [Yeshayah 6:3]. Faith is the basis of *yirah*. The thought that His glory fills the entire earth, and Hashem is the Creator of all things, and He dominates the entire Creation, inevitably increases one's *yiras Shamayim (sifrei kodesh)*.

- Why did Hashem choose to speak to Moshe Rabbeinu from a bush? To demonstrate that there is no place void of His existence, including a lowly bush (*Midrash Shemos* 2:5).

- What is *yirah*? It is the acceptance of the yoke of Torah and mitzvos—there is a Master Who rules over us. This knowledge must be clear, as the verse says (Divrei Hayamim I 28:9), "Know your forefather's God, and serve Him with a full heart" (*Reishis Choch-mah*, "*Shaar Hayirah*," ch. 1).

- Hashem continually grants us the gift of life. As we say in *tefillah*, "We thank You for our lives, which are in Your hands, and for our *neshamos*, which are at Your command." We see from this section of *tefillah* [*Modim*] that we are constantly dependent on the Creator for our existence. This is alluded to by the Sages' interpretation of the verse, "The whole *ne-shamah* will praise the Lord" [Tehillim 150:6]—we must praise Hashem for every breath we take (*Toras Chaim, Bava Kama* 16a).

- "For the ways of man are before Hashem's eyes, and He ponders all his goings" (Mishlei 5:21).

- "Hashem looks down from heaven, He beholds all the sons of man.... He Who fashions their hearts alike, Who considers all their deeds" (Tehillim 33:13-15).

- Every single transgression ever committed by any individual is recorded in a *sefer* (*Avos* 2:1, and Rabbeinu Yonah).

- "...Know the God of your father, and serve Him with a perfect heart and a willing mind; for Hashem searches all hearts, and understands all imagination and thought; if you seek Him, He will be found by you, but if you forsake Him, he will cast you off forever" (Divrei Hayamim I 28:9).

- "If you seek it [*yiras Shamayim*] like silver, and search for it as for hidden treasures, then you will understand the fear of Hashem..." (Mishlei 2:4-5).

- One must clearly believe that Hashem watches over his actions (*sifrei kodesh*).

- There are 248 limbs in the human body; they correspond to the 248 positive mitzvos. Every limb calls out to man, "Do mitzvos so that you will merit to live!" (*Tanchuma, Ki Seitzei* 2).

- "For every mitzvah a person performs, he receives a heavenly advocate, and for every sin a person commits, he receives a heavenly prosecutor " (*Avos* 4:13).

- "For His eyes are on the ways of man, and He sees all his goings" (Iyov 34:21).

- True *yirah* will become permanently ingrained in one's consciousness by consistent pondering this concept: Hashem is omnipresent. King David prayed to Hashem, "Teach me your ways, unite my heart to love Your name" (*Mesilas Yesharim*, ch. 25).

- Achievements that required many years of effort by the *yetzer hatov* can be destroyed in a few seconds by the *yetzer hara* (*Pesikta Rabbati* 9).

The following are statements that awaken one to do *teshuvah*:

- Hashem said to Israel: "My children, do *teshuvah* while the Gates of Repentance are still open!" (*Midrash Shachar Tov Tehillim* 17).

- "It is preferable that a man accept the yoke during his youth" (Eichah 3:27).

- "Your clothes should be constantly white" (Koheles 9:8).

- "Do *teshuvah* one day before your death" (*Avos* 2:15).

- Do not say, "I will do it tomorrow," for "you do not know what tomorrow will bring" (Mishlei 27:1).

- Punctilious people perform mitzvos at the earliest possible moment (*Pesachim* 4a).

- Today they are to be performed, and tomorrow the reward will be received (*Avodah Zarah* 3a).

- "Whatever your hand finds to do, do it with your strength, for there is no work, or device, or knowledge, or wisdom, in *Sheol*" (Koheles 9:10).

- What man cannot accomplish while Hashem supplies him with strength and free choice, he will certainly not accomplish when he is in the grave (*Mesilas Yesharim*, ch. 4).

- One who did not perform kind deeds during his life cannot perform them after his life (ibid.).

- One who did not make a personal accounting during his life will certainly be unable to make it after his life (ibid.).

- One who did not become wise during his life will not become wise in the grave (ibid).

- *Teshuvah*, like all other mitzvos, must be performed with joy. There is no greater joy than the joy of doing *teshuvah* (*Shaarei Teshuvah*, ch. 4, section 9).

The statements below will strengthen one's ability to concentrate on the study of Torah and not become distracted during the study of Torah:

- Hashem overlooked idolatry, licentious relations, and bloodshed, but He did not tolerate *bitul Torah* (Yerushalmi, *Chagigah*, ch. 1, halachah 7).

- One who pauses from study (for idle chatter—Rashi) is punished by being fed burning coals (*Avodah Zarah* 3b and *Chagigah* 12b).

- The study of Torah is more valuable than all the mitzvos. The Talmud Yerushalmi explains that one word of Torah is more valuable than the fulfillment of all the mitzvos (*Peah*, ch. 1, halachah 1).

- Anyone who is capable of Torah study and does not apply himself to this study is considered to have disgraced the name of Hashem (*Sanhedrin* 99a).

- One who refrains from studying Torah eventually falls into Gehenom (*Baba Basra* 79a).

- One should approach the study of Torah with the same determination with which an ox pulls a yoke and a donkey transports a load (*Tana Devei Eliyahu Zitra*, ch. 1).

- "The words of Torah that emanate from your mouth are more valuable than a treasure of gold and silver" (Tehillim 119:9).

Chapter Ten

Approaching Teshuvah—IV

The Third Step: Teshuvah for "Light" Transgressions

The *teshuvah* process should begin with correcting transgressions that can be easily overcome. There are many habitual sins that do not entrap people with the promise of pleasure and that do not, therefore, severely test one's resolve. With this approach, the taste of victory will strengthen the penitent's conviction that he can continue in the *teshuvah* process:

The Gemara says[1] that the punishment meted out to a person who does not wear white *tzitzis* is more severe than the punishment for not wearing the *techeiles* string in his *tzitzis*. The reason is it is relatively easy to acquire white strings, but more difficult to acquire *techeiles* strings. This gemara teaches us the concept that the severity of a transgression is proportional to the difficulty involved in fulfilling

---

1. *Menachos* 43b.

the mitzvah. Mitzvos that are easy to fulfill carry more severe punishments than mitzvos that are difficult to fulfill. For example, a person who does not pray with a minyan due to the difficulty involved in getting out of bed in the morning deserves a lighter punishment than a person who speaks during *tefillah*.

It follows that the obligation to do *teshuvah* for transgressions that can be easily avoided is greater than the obligation to do *teshuvah* for transgressions that are difficult to avoid. R. Yisrael Salanter wrote, in *Ohr Yisrael*,[2] that one should first attempt to do *teshuvah* for "light" transgressions: "One must make a personal accounting and resolve to avoid sins, in all areas of Halachah, that are easy to avoid. The penitent will thus be credited with having achieved *teshuvah* for most of his sins, because sins are not measured numerically, but qualitatively—the transgression of a mitzvah that can be easily avoided is considered to be a more serious sin than several transgressions that are more difficult to avoid."

---

2. Ch. 16.

Chapter Eleven

Approaching Teshuvah—V

Resolutions

Anyone who attempts to make a resolution to disassociate himself from a specific transgression will experience internal turmoil and be lured by reason and emotion to abandon his efforts. The *yetzer hara* is a truly ferocious opponent and unwilling to surrender territory to the *yetzer hatov*. This concept is alluded to in the incident of Yaakov's struggle with Esav's guardian angel. As the verse says, "An angel struggled with him until daybreak" (Bereishis 32:25). Yaakov was successful in this struggle. "And he [the angel] saw that he could not defeat him [Yaakov]..." (ibid., 26). Yaakov's victory over this angel became permanently imbedded in the soul of the Jewish People; his victory enables us to conquer our *yetzer hara*. This potential may only be achieved by implementing the weapon that enabled Yaakov to vanquish his enemy, the trait of *emes* (truthfulness).

A truthful man keeps his word; truthfulness is essential to strengthening one's will to carry out resolutions. In addition, a person must use carefully planned strategy, as it says, "With strategy he makes war" (Mishlei 20:18). The strategy that strengthens the trait of truthfulness is the understanding of the severity of sin and the great obligation imposed on us to serve Hashem. Together, these two concepts will enable the penitent to implement his resolve.

After strengthening his resolve through study and contemplation, he is ready to make his resolutions.

Summary

The main effort after recognizing one's sins is to strengthen his resolve through studying the severity of sin and the great value of mitzvos; afterwards, one should resolve with great sincerity to change his evil ways.

Chapter Twelve

Introspection

AS WE NOTED in chapter 7, certain transgressions cannot be easily identified. Only intense self-analysis and introspection will reveal that some behaviors that we understand to be "permitted" are actually prohibited. As it says in Eichah, "Let us search our ways and come back to Hashem" (3:40). The sins requiring the most analysis are transgressions against one's fellowman and transgressions which stem from negative character traits, because it is inherently difficult for one to recognize his own faults.[1] This is implied in the Rambam: "Just as one must do *teshuvah* for transgressions committed through physical acts, one also must reassess his character traits and correct the negative ones."[2]

One must, therefore, do *teshuvah* for feeling anger, hatred, jealousy, frivolity, pride, and desire for food. One should

---

1. See also *Palgei Mayim*, Eichah 3:40.
2. *Hilchos Teshuvah*, ch. 7, halachah 3.

further reassess the extent to which he fulfills all the halachos and mitzvos and their many ramifications as specified in
the *Shulchan Aruch*, for example *tefillah*, Shabbos, Yom Tov,
lashon hara, and the mitzvah of washing one's hands.

Needless to say, a person who is not knowledgeable
about Halachah will have great difficulty in recognizing and
identifying his transgressions. The Orchos Tzaddikim de-
clares: One who is not well versed in the mitzvos will frequently
stumble; such a person will sin all his life and be unaware of
it.[3] The long-term answer to this problem is to begin an
intensive program of study which will eventually familiarize
him with a large portion of Halachah. What can such a
person do however when he is confronted with the imminent
approach of Yom Kippur? How can he determine whether his
actions are permitted if he does not know the Halachah? It
would seem, at first glance, that the portals of *teshuvah* are
sealed for him.

Rabbeinu Yonah prescribes the solution to this problem:
A penitent who resolves to familiarize himself with Halachah and follow the guidance of the Rabbis is credited with
having fulfilled the entire Torah, including those mitzvos of
which he is totally ignorant. This is similar to the decision
that the Jewish People made at Har Sinai when they de-
clared, "We will do and we will understand" (Shemos 24:7),
which resulted in their receiving much merit.[4]

In this way, a penitent who is apparently entrapped by
ignorance of mitzvos can do *teshuvah* swiftly and receive
untold merit and rewards for doing so. The Sages[5] asked
about the verse, "And the Jewish People went and they
performed" (Shemos 12:28)— "Does this mean that they

---

3. "*Shaar Hateshuvah*."

4. *Shaarei Teshuvah*, ch. 2, letter 10.

5. *Mechilta Shemos* 12:28.

immediately performed all the mitzvos? Rather, the verse
teaches us that once the Jewish People decided to fulfill all
the mitzvos that Hashem commanded, the Torah regarded
them as if they had actually fulfilled them."[6]

---

6. *Orchos Tzaddikim*; also see *Avos*, Rabbeinu Yonah, 3:9.

Chapter Thirteen

Atonement of Yom Kippur—I

The Obligation to Do Teshuvah

The Ramban's opinion is that the obligation to do *te-shuva* begins prior to Yom Kippur,[1] as the verse says, "You will purify yourselves from all your sins *before* Hashem [the day of Hashem]" (Vayikra 16:30). This is the reason why the *poskim* have determined that one should confess his sins immediately prior to sundown on *erev* Yom Kippur, an obligation we fulfill by reciting the *Tefillah Zakah*.[2]

The Rambam states, however, that *teshuvah* must be performed during Yom Kippur: "Yom Kippur is the time when individuals and the entire Jewish People must do *teshuvah*. It is an opportune time for *teshuvah*, when the Jewish People receive atonement for their sins. Everyone is therefore obligated to do *teshuvah* and confess his sins during Yom

---

1. *Yoma* 97b, see Rabbeinu Nissim.
2. *Chayei Adam* 144:20.

Kippur."³ Similarly, Rabbeinu Yonah writes, "It is a positive mitzvah to awaken oneself to do *teshuvah* during Yom Kippur—'You will purify yourselves from all your sins before Hashem' [Vayikra 16:30]. This verse warns us to purify ourselves before Hashem through *teshuvah*."⁴

The words of the Rambam imply that it is not a positive mitzvah to do *teshuvah* during Yom Kippur—the Rambam says that Yom Kippur is an opportune time for *teshuvah*. If doing *teshuvah* during Yom Kippur was an explicit mitzvah, the Rambam would not have described Yom Kippur as "an opportune time." Furthermore, he does not include the obligation to do *teshuvah* on Yom Kippur in the list of positive mitzvos he compiled. Therefore, the Rambam's logic seems to be that Yom Kippur only atones for a person's sins if he does *teshuvah*; since Hashem appointed this day for atonement, we may deduce that anyone who wants to be pardoned for his sins must do *teshuvah*.

The Sages say that during the ten days prior to Yom Kippur Hashem clears the path to *teshuvah* by, in a manner of speech, coming closer to us. There is therefore no greater desecration than to refrain from *teshuvah* during these days. This is analogous to the following midrash: A band of thieves were captured and jailed. They dug a tunnel through which they all, except one, escaped. When the officer of the jail discovered the escape, he was startled to find one of the prisoners still in his cell. Infuriated by the sight, he began to strike the lone prisoner fiercely. He said to him, "The way to escape is open to you. How is it that you did not escape?"⁵

Rabbeinu Yonah adds that a sinner who refrains from *teshuvah* when he is given the opportunity will face severe

---

3. *Hilchos Teshuvah*, ch. 2, halachah 7.
4. *Shaarei Teshuvah*, ch. 2, letter 5.
5. *Midrash Koheles Rabbah* 7:30.

punishment for not having taken advantage of his means of escape—*teshuvah*.

It is the trait of a *talmid chacham* to do *teshuvah* swiftly. As the Sages said, "If you see a *talmid chacham* commit a transgression during the evening, do not think badly of him the next day, for he has surely done *teshuvah*."[6]

---

6. *Berachos* 19a.

Chapter Fourteen

Atonement of Yom Kippur—II

Interpersonal Transgressions

The Rambam writes, "Transgressions committed against one's fellowman, for example, theft or causing damage, are not forgiven unless the transgressor first monetarily reimburses the damaged party and subsequently succeeds in appeasing him. Even though he has reimbursed him monetarily, he must appease him and ask for forgiveness."[1] The Rambam adds that even this is not sufficient. He writes: "Even though he has reimbursed him for the damage he caused him, the transgressor will not be forgiven by Hashem until he confesses his sins and resolves to refrain from repeating this transgression in the future."[2]

The Beis Elokim writes, "A person who has committed a transgression against his fellowman and has not yet reim-

1. *Hilchos Teshuvah,* ch. 2, halachah 9.
2. Ibid., ch. 1, halachah 1.

bursed him monetarily is regarded as a *baal teshuvah* if he merely resolves to reimburse him in the future."[3] The source for this ruling is the following halachah: A man who marries a woman on the condition that he is a perfect *tzaddik* is considered to be legally married to her, because it is possible that he resolved to do *teshuvah*.[4] From this ruling we may infer that the resolve to do *teshuvah* transforms any sinner into a *baal teshuvah*, even one who transgressed against his fellowman.

Similarly, one who insulted his fellowman and has not yet had the opportunity to ask him for forgiveness, but resolves to do so at the first opportunity, may be regarded as a *baal teshuvah* if he has repented. It is questionable whether such an individual will be atoned for by Yom Kippur, or whether the atonement will be delayed until he asks the other party for forgiveness.

---

3. "*Shaar Hateshuvah*," ch. 2.
4. *Kiddushin* 49b.

Chapter Fifteen

Atonement of Yom Kippur—III

THE RAMBAM WRITES, "Since the Beis Hamikdash is destroyed, and we do not have an altar nor atonement, we only have *teshuvah*....[1] The day of Yom Kippur alone atones for the sins of those who do *teshuvah*, as the verse says, 'This day will atone for you...' [Vayikra 16:30]. However, Yom Kippur will not atone for the sins of one who has committed transgressions that are punishable with *kareis* and death at the hands of the *Beis Din* (intentional sins), even though he has done *teshuvah*. Rather, atonement for this type of sinner will occur only after tribulations visit him. As it says, 'I will command the rod for your sins, and the plague for your iniquities' [Tehillim 89:33]. An individual who refrained from fulfilling a positive mitzvah and subsequently did *teshuvah* is atoned for by Yom Kippur alone."[2] The reason why a transgressor of negative mitzvos is not purified from his sins

---

1. *Hilchos Teshuvah*, ch. 1, halachah 3.
2. Ibid., halachos 3-4.

sins by merely doing *teshuvah* (even though he is regarded as a *tzaddik*, as explained in chapter 14) is because the sin that he committed contaminated his soul to the extent that *teshuvah* alone is not sufficient to purify him.[3]

The Maharal explains that *teshuvah* draws the penitent closer to Hashem, but does not purify his soul from the contamination caused by sin. *Teshuvah* suspends judgment, while Yom Kippur atones for sin. The day itself purifies the sinner from the *tumah* that infected his soul, as it says, "This day will atone for you to purify you" (Vayikra 16:30).[4]

Hashem Himself purifies the soul of the sinner from the *tumah*. As it says, "Joyous are you, Israel, for our Father in Heaven purifies you."[5] *Teshuvah* and Yom Kippur, in conjunction with the physical effects of fasting, uplift the soul of the sinner to spiritual ascension, and in turn cause him to become purified from the spiritual impurity that pervaded his soul at the time of the sin.

This explains why the *seir le'Azazel* (scapegoat) atones for the light sins of the Jewish People even without *teshuvah*. The *kohen gadol* was able to uplift the spiritual consciousness of the entire Jewish People to such an extent that they became like angels, free from the *yetzer hara* and so close to Hashem that they felt sincere regret over their past sins.

---

3. *Beis Elokim*, "*Shaar Hateshuvah*," ch. 5.

4. *Nesiv Hateshuvah*, ch. 3.

5. *Yoma* 85b.

Chapter Sixteen

Teshuvah for Involuntary Transgressions

ONE WHO UNINTENTIONALLY violates a mitzvah that carries the punishment of *kareis* when it is intentionally violated must offer a *korban chatas*.[1] He must do *teshuvah* and confess when he brings his *korban*. This procedure offers proof that one must do *teshuvah* even for unintentional sins. For this reason, the word "*chatanu*" appears in the confession recital; it refers to sins committed unintentionally.

The Beis Elokim points out that unintentional sins require atonement because they occur as a result of a low degree of *yiras Shamayim*. One who is truly fearful of transgressing mitzvos would never even commit involuntary sins. The fact that a person sinned unwittingly demonstrates that he was momentarily distracted from *yiras Shamayim*. He must do *teshuvah* for this, since the degree of *yiras Shamayim* that

---

1. As explained in *Hilchos Teshuvah*, ch. 1, halachah 1.

one maintains is under the control of the individual.

Although actions not explicitly prohibited by the Torah are, by definition, permissible, the attitude of a person who has *yiras Shamayim* should be that before he carries out an action, he must first ascertain beyond doubt that it is permitted. Had *yiras Shamayim* permeated the individual's consciousness, the sin would have never occurred.

It is advisable to adopt the trait of carefulness as customary practice, since this will help prevent unintentional sins from occurring. With this concept in mind we may appreciate why the Sages stress so strongly the importance of remembering the Torah one has learned.[2] Memory, or forgetfulness, can normally be controlled. Forgetfulness leads to unintentional sin.[3]

---

2. *Avos* 3:10.
3. *Beis Elokim*, "*Shaar Hateshuvah*," ch. 1.

Chapter Seventeen

Transgressions After Teshuvah—I

THE RAMBAM WRITES that the confession recital should include the words, "I will never repeat this transgression again."[1] He adds that *teshuvah* should be performed with the awareness that the penitent is giving testimony about himself in the presence of Hashem, for this will prevent him from repeating the transgression in the future.[2] Rabbeinu Tam writes similarly in *Sefer Hayashar*, "*Teshuvah*, if performed in such a manner, will ensure the penitent will not repeat his transgression, for no man would lie in Hashem's presence."

The Beis Elokim's opinion is that *teshuvah* is valid even if the penitent did not resolve to refrain from repeating the transgression in the future.[3] Perhaps we may rely on his opinion in the case of a person who finds it difficult to make

---

1. *Hilchos Teshuvah*, halachah 1.
2. Ibid., ch. 2, halachah 2.
3. "*Shaar Hateshuvah*," ch. 6.

resolutions; as long as he ceases to commit the sin temporarily, his *teshuvah* will be valid.

Most *poskim*, however, are of the opinion that all four components of *teshuvah* are essential. If so, what should a person do if he doubts he will be able to refrain from repeating the transgression in the future?

The Beis Elokim's opinion[4] is the fact that the penitent repeats his transgression does not demonstrate retroactively that his original *teshuvah* was insincere and, therefore, invalid. He explains that the essential component of *teshuvah* is to feel regret, which this individual did feel. Due to the subtle enticements of the *yetzer hara* he repeated the transgression, which does not reflect in any way on the original act of *teshuvah*.[5]

This is analogous to a smoker who decides to quit smoking time after time. The resolve to quit the habit usually stems from the realization that smoking is unhealthy. The smoker is only able to think logically about smoking at times when his desire to smoke temporarily slackens. When the desire returns, his resolution and objectivity disappear in a cloud of smoke. His decision was honest and sincere, despite the fact that he was not able to carry it through. *Teshuvah*'s essential component is regret; therefore, regression does not contradict the good intentions that accompanied his *teshuvah*.

4. "*Shaar Hateshuvah*," ch. 6.

5. This subject is discussed in *Kochvei Ohr*, R. Itzaleh Peterburger, ch. 6.

Chapter Eighteen

Transgressions After Teshuvah—II

A PENITENT SHOULD not be deterred from doing *teshuvah* by the following thought: "I have made many resolutions in the past, but I have not succeeded in keeping them. It would be a meaningless gesture for me to make any more resolutions, because I will probably fail to fulfill them, as I have failed in the past." This line of reasoning is erroneous. When a person considers *teshuvah*, he should not think about the past or the future. Doing so will only weaken his resolve. *Teshuvah* must be done in the present, and if the penitent feels strong and determined to succeed, he should make whatever resolution he feels will help him.

One may feel, even at the moment of *teshuvah*, that he lacks the power to refrain from sin if faced with temptation. Still, he honestly hopes not to sin again, he prays to avoid the *nisayon*, and he is prepared to run from temptation. He builds "fences" to protect himself and resolves to strengthen himself in the future. Such a person is considered to have begun the process of *teshuvah*.

The Chovos Halevavos writes, "A person who feels regret for his sins and is successful in refraining from sin when confronted by his *yetzer hara* is on the path to *teshuvah*. Even if he feels that he is still attracted to the transgression and sometimes ensnared by his physical self, he is considered to be on the path to *teshuvah*. His *teshuvah*, however, is not regarded as complete until he succeeds in uprooting the desire to sin from his being."[1] From this we learn that even a person who feels he would like to refrain from committing transgressions, but knows he would succumb to temptation were an opportunity to arise, is still considered to be on the path to *teshuvah*.

The Beis Elokim's opinion is that, unlike other mitzvos, if a penitent performs the mitzvah of *teshuvah* incompletely, he is still credited with partial merit.[2] This concept offers strong encouragement to a penitent who feels insecure about his chance of success. He should do as much as possible, since he can be assured of merit for all his efforts.

It is better to do *teshuvah* and transgress than never to do *teshuvah* at all. Even a person who does *teshuvah* and later repeats the transgression will receive Divine assistance in his attempts to conform to the mitzvos. He may not achieve complete atonement this Yom Kippur, but his persistence will eventually merit complete atonement. As the Sages say, "One who wants to become purified receives Divine assistance."[3]

---

1. "*Shaar Hateshuvah*," ch. 2.

2. "*Shaar Hateshuvah*," ch. 12.

3. *Yoma* 38b.

Chapter Nineteen

Atonement Without Korbanos

THE RAMBAM WRITES that in our days, when we have only *teshuvah* and the day of Yom Kippur to atone for sins, we may atone for transgressions without the offering of the *seir hamishtaleach*.[1] When there is no Beis Hamikdash, even an involuntary sin that carries the punishment of *kareis* may be atoned for without offering a *korban*.

The fact that the *korban* was an essential component of atonement when the Beis Hamikdash stood and is not essential in our day requires explanation.

The Beis Elokim explains that the existence of the Beis Hamikdash causes the Divine Shechinah to dwell closer to the Jewish People, which in turn intensifies their *yiras Shamayim*, which increases awareness of the inherent severity of sin.[2] Since the Beis Hamikdash was destroyed, we have lacked

---

1. *Hilchos Teshuvah*, ch. 1, halachah 3.
2. "*Shaar Hateshuvah*," ch. 2.

this increased awareness. In these times, the Shechinah hides in our midst, as the verse says, "And I will surely hide My face on that day because of all the evils which they shall have perpetrated, for they have turned to other gods" (Devarim 31:18).

A person who transgressed a mitzvah when the Beis Hamikdash stood was judged more harshly than one who does so after the destruction of the Beis Hamikdash. There are two reasons why this is so:

1) An offense committed while the Beis Hamikdash stood, a time when an overwhelming sense of spirituality pervaded the consciousness of the Jewish People, demonstrated that the sinner was not ensnared by the *yetzer hara*, but either chose to sin or was extremely neglectful in avoiding sin.

2) An offense committed during the days when the Beis Hamikdash stood and the Shechinah was openly revealed was interpreted an act of insolence against the Shechinah.

We may now understand why a *korban* was required to atone for sins committed while the Beis Hamikdash stood, but not essential to atone for sins committed after the destruction of the Beis Hamikdash. Simply speaking, sins committed while the Beis Hamikdash stood were considerably more severe than sins committed after its destruction, requiring a greater form of atonement.

Chapter Twenty

"Tzaddikim Cannot Stand in the Place Where Baalei Teshuvah Stand"

IT SHOULD BE made clear that the *baal teshuvah* referred to in the statement of the Sages above has also fulfilled all the levels of attainment that characterize a *tzaddik* as enumerated in *Mesilas Yesharim*.[1] The question, then, is this: who is greater, the *tzaddik* who has transgressed nothing more than minor sins, as the verse says, "For there is no man who is so righteous in this world that he does only good and never sins" (Koheles 7:20), or the *baal teshuvah*, who has reached the level of righteousness of the *tzaddik*?

According to the Chovos Halevavos[2] such a *baal teshuvah* is superior to a *tzaddik* because he is less inclined to feel pride at his spiritual attainments. A *baal teshuvah* who has specifically undergone the twenty steps of *teshuvah* has reached

---

1. Ch. 13.
2. Ch. 8.

an unprecedented level of humility. A *tzaddik*, however, faces the danger of haughtiness, while a *baal teshuvah* does not.

A *baal teshuvah* who committed a transgression that carries either the death penalty by Beis Din or *kareis*, or one that involves a *chillul Hashem*, is not considered greater than a *tzaddik* who never transgressed.[3]

According to the Beis Elokim, a *baal teshuvah* is greater than a *tzaddik* who is righteous by nature, one who is inclined towards the proper path, walks on it, and is consequently considered a total *tzaddik*. When a *baal teshuvah* who must constantly do battle with his *yetzer hara* and overcome its temptation is compared with such a natural *tzaddik*, it is the *baal teshuvah* who surpasses—as it says, "the reward is according to the effort" (*Avos* 5:26).

However, some *tzaddikim* are *not* naturally inclined towards the proper path. They must wage constantly battle the *yetzer hara*. Of these, the Sages have said that the greater the person, the greater his *yetzer*. Such *tzaddikim* surpass the *baal teshuvah*. They succeed because of their constant effort and vigilance, day in and day out, and their superior love and fear of God. These *tzaddikim* do not stumble in any transgression, either serious or light, except for the shortcomings that no one can escape by virtue of his being human. Such *tzaddikim* surpass both the total *baal teshuvah* and the natural *tzaddik* (*Beis Elokim*, ch. 4).

Most likely, the Beis Elokim and the Chovos Halevavos do not contradict each other. The Chovos Halevavos would also admit that a *tzaddik* who is naturally inclined toward sin yet overcomes temptation surpasses a *baal teshuvah*. It is also possible that the Beis Elokim will grant that someone who has committed a serious transgression and has repented does not surpass the *tzaddik* who has never sinned.

---

3. See Rambam, *Hilchos Teshuvah*, ch. 1, halachah 4, and *Chovos Halevavos*, ch. 8.